Natural Ellipse

2002 Tokyo, Japan

Architect: *Masaki Endoh+Masahiro Ikeda*
Photos: *Hiroyasu Sakaguchi*

ナチュラルエリップス
2002　東京
建築家　遠藤政樹+池田昌弘

ナチュラルエリップス
Natural Ellipse

目　次

- ◇住宅写真　　　　　　　　　　　　　　　　4-19
- ◇図面　　　　　　　　　　　　　　　　　　22
- ◇施工写真、エスキース、ディティール　　24, 30, 34
- ◇解説　　遠藤政樹
  - 小さいこと、東京に住むこと、特殊であること　36
  - 円山町、エリップスであること　　　　　　　38
  - ＦＲＰであること　　　　　　　　　　　　　40
  - スチールであること　　　　　　　　　　　　42
  - ナチュラルであること　　　　　　　　　　　44
  - 未知なるものへ　　　　　　　　　　　　　　44

Contents

- ◇Photos of the Ellipse　　　　　　　　　　　　4-19
- ◇Architectural plans　　　　　　　　　　　　　22
- ◇Photos of the Construction, Drawings, Detail　24, 30, 34
- ◇Text by Masaki Endoh
  - Being Small, Living in Tokyo and Being Unique　37
  - Maruyamacho – Being an Ellipse　　　　　　39
  - Being FRP　　　　　　　　　　　　　　　　41
  - Being Steel　　　　　　　　　　　　　　　　43
  - Being Natural　　　　　　　　　　　　　　　45
  - To the Unknown　　　　　　　　　　　　　　45

ナチュラルエリップス外観。北側と東側の2面を道路に接する。スチールの楕円リングのシルエットが外観に残る。外壁は珪酸カルシウム板の上に難燃仕様を施したＦＲＰ仕上げ。

Exterior view of Natural Ellipse. The north facade and the east facade face the street. Signs of elliptical rings slightly remain on the surface. The exterior wall is layered with FRP(which is reformed on unflammable) on top of the calcium silicate board.

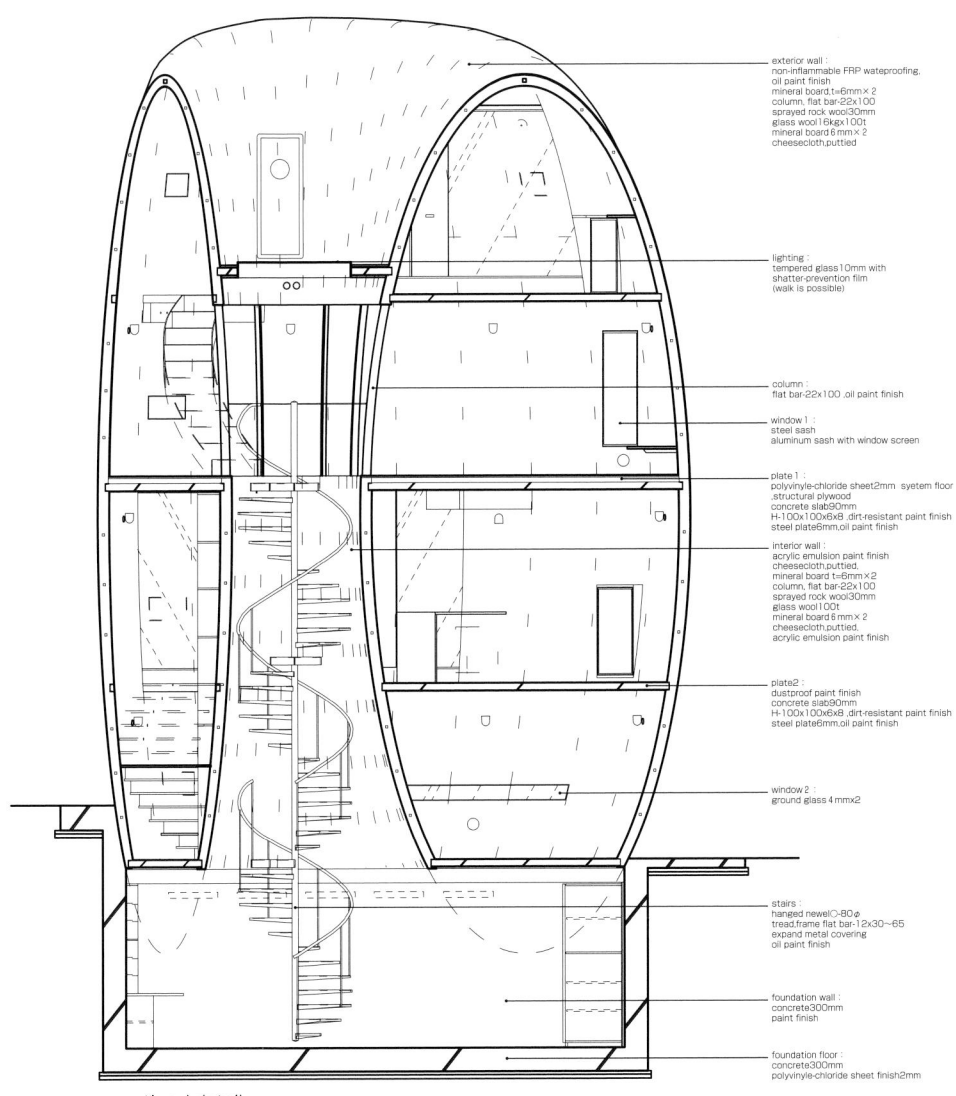

sectional detail

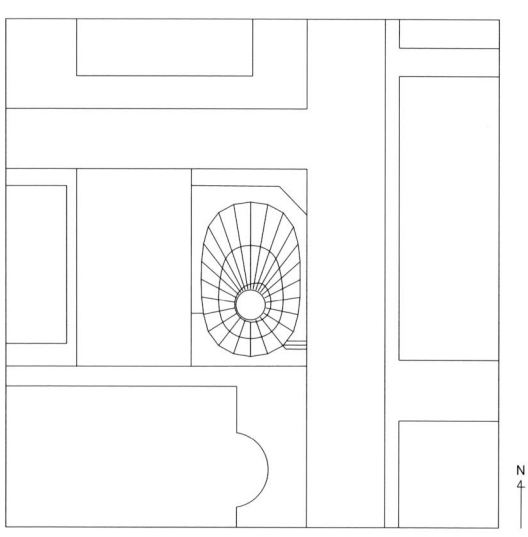

site

▶ 夜景。東京のネオンサインを反射する。中央のくぼみ部分がトップライト。そこは上下を繋ぐ螺旋階段である。地階と3階4階がオーナー住居。1階と2階が賃貸住居。

Night view. Reflection of the neon signs of Tokyo. The central well is a sky light. It is a spiral staircase that connects the top and bottom. The ground floor and the 3rd-4th floors constitute the owner's residence. The 1st and 2nd floors constitute the rental part.

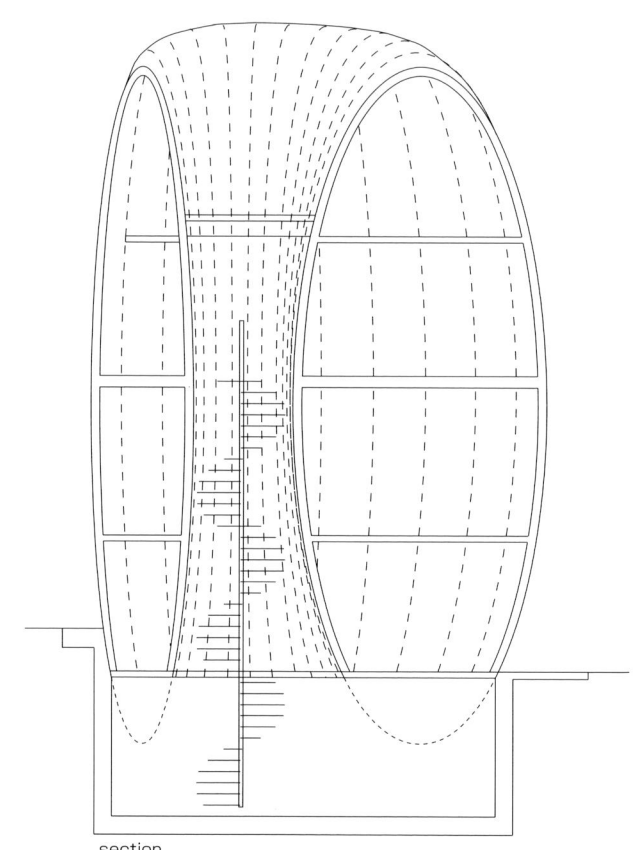

section

賃貸部2階リビング。中央が螺旋階段の筒。ここでも、うっすらと楕円リングの痕跡が残っている。賃貸住居は、この筒のさらに外側を、回り階段で上り下りをする2重構造。右奥がシャワー室。その手前がキッチン。

Rental part's living area on the 2nd Floor. The center is the spiral stair's shaft. Signs of an elliptical ring slightly remain here. The rental residence is on the outside of this shaft and constitutes a double structure that goes up and down of the circular staircase. On the right side rear is the shower room. Right in front is the kitchen.

地階。浮いた螺旋階段。矩形の地下室に、不定形のナチュラルエリップスの本体がすっぽりはまっている構成がわかる。

Ground Floor. The floating spiral staircase. The main body of the Natural Ellipse's infinite form is snuggly fitted into the rectangular shaped basement structure.

3階リビングスペース。トップライトのある螺旋階段を中心に家具が配置される。小さな面積にかかわらず、丸い壁のため、大きく感じさせてくれる。左が4階ロフトへのよじ捩れた階段。右がキッチン。中央が予備のためのトイレ。

Living space on the 3rd floor. The furnitures are arranged centered around the spiral staircase possessing a sky light. Regardless of the small area, it is made to feel larger due to the round walls. On the left is the staircase that spins to the 4th floor loft. The right is the kitchen. The center is the reserve restroom.

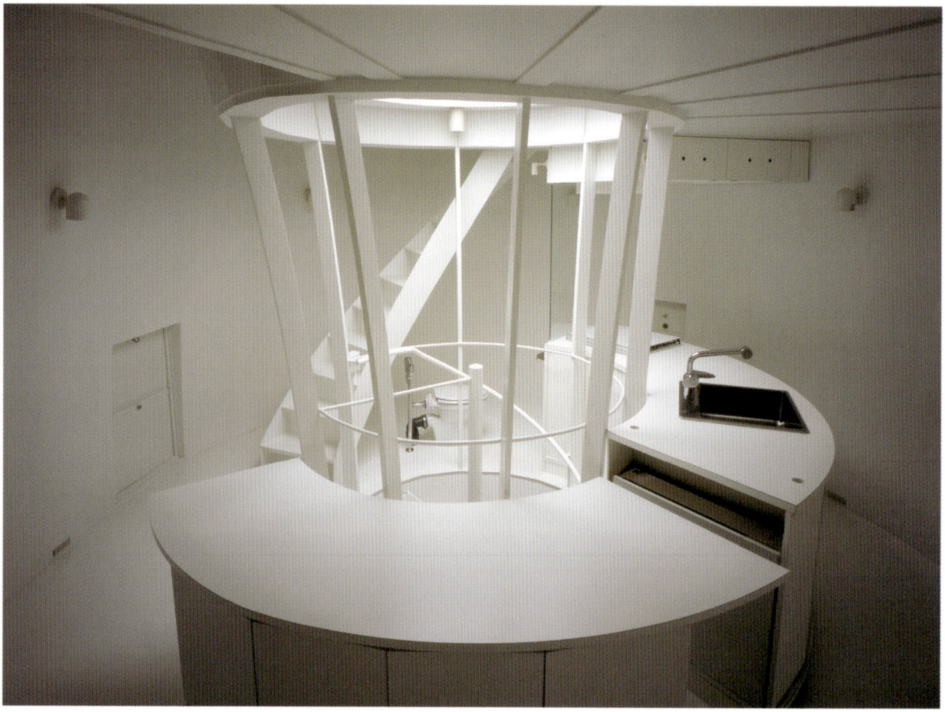

▲ 手前に移動式ダイニングテーブルがある場合の3階リビング。天井は鉄板化粧型枠仕上げにペンキ仕上げ。楕円リングの繋ぎとして、放射状に伸びる梁があらわれている。

At the front is the the 3rd floor living area with a movable dining table. The ceiling is paint finished on steel a mold form. The beam that expands radially acts as a tie to the elliptical ring.

◀ 地階から見上げ。この螺旋階段の筒は、僅かに変形し、楕円リングの一部で構成される。左がオーナー住居玄関。光の筒であり、風の通り道であり、生活の主導線である。

Looking up from the basement. The cylinder of this spiral staircase slightly transforms, and is composed partly from the elliptical ring. The left side is the owner's residence's entrance. The cylinder performs as a path for the light and wind, and the main route of the building.

▲ 螺旋階段見下げ。床は長尺塩ビシート仕上げ。壁は珪酸カルシウム板の上ペンキ仕上げ。

Looking down the spiral staircase. The floor is finished with lengthy PVC sheeting. The wall is paint finished on calcium silicate boards.

キッチンテーブルに正対する。
現代的だが茶の手前を感じさせる。

*Opposite of the kitchen table.
Although it is modern, it brings up the
peaceful atmosphere of a tea ceremony.*

3階スペースから階段を昇ると寝室ゾーンへ。

*From the 3rd floor, going up the staircase
and towards the bedroom area.*

▲ 4階ロフトの一番手前の洗面脱衣室を見上げる。その奥が浴室。さらにその奥に寝室。
中央螺旋階段を立体的に取り巻くように数珠状に配置された部屋配置。
Looking up from the front of the 4th floor loft's vanity dressing room. The back is the bathroom. And behind this is the bedroom.
The room arrangement is placed in a moniliform surrounding the central spiral staircase three-dimensionally.

▲ 洗面脱衣室とトップライト
Vanity dressing room and high side window

▲ 4階ロフトの寝室へは、右のはしごを使っても上下移動が可能となっている。数珠状に連なった部屋配置は最後に再び空間的に一体化して終わっている。
It is possible to move up and down to the 4th floor loft bedroom with the ladder on the right. The monoliform room arrangement terminates again in spatial integration in the end.

▶ 浴室から洗面脱衣室を見る。浴槽、床、壁ともにFRP仕上げ。上の壁には横長のハイサイド窓がある。

Vanity dressing room seen from the bathroom. Bath, floors, and walls are finished in FRP. The wall above has a wide high side window.

▶ トップライトの屋上テラス。そこから室内を見る。床は強化ガラス仕上げ。このテラスのところで、楕円リングが外から内へひっくりかえっていく。右上が洗面脱衣室からの入口戸。

Roof terrace of the sky light. Looking to the inside of the room. The floor is covered with a tempered glass finish. On this terrace, the elliptical ring is inverted from the outside to the inside. The upper right is the entrance door from the vanity dressing room.

▲ トップライトテラスから下を見る。
Looking down from the roof terrace of the sky light.

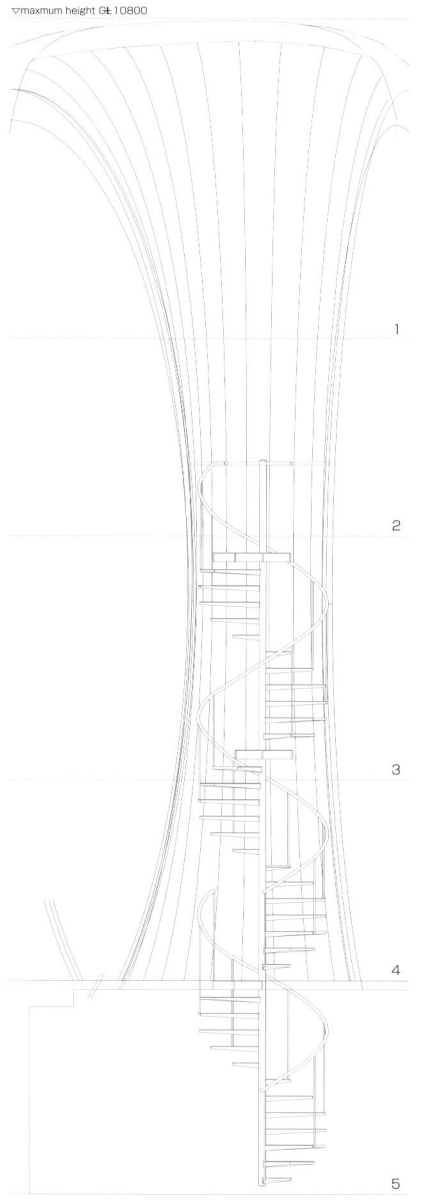

▽maxmum height GL+10800

◀左：内側楕円リングと螺旋階段。
　右：楕円リングスケルトン。全部で24個の
　　　楕円リングからなる。

Left: Inner oval ring and spiral staircase.
Right: Elliptical ring skeleton.
It consists of 24 elliptical rings in total.

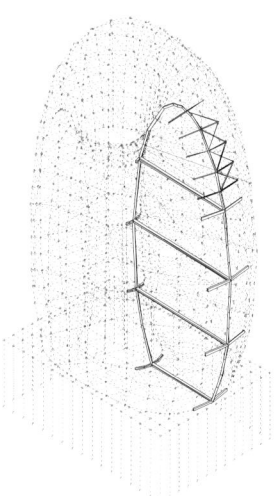

axonometric

stair detail
1 4FL GL+7200
2 3FL GL+4990
3 2FL GL+2250
4 1FL GL+0
5 BFL GL-2400

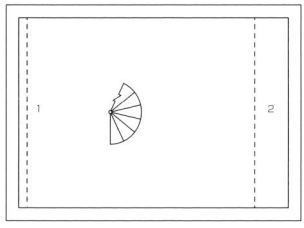

Basement Plan

1 bookshelf
2 closet

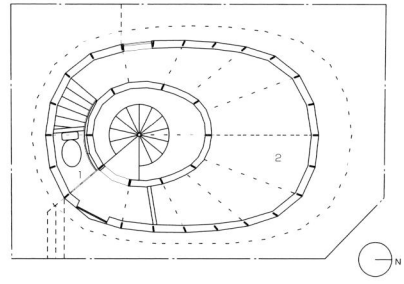

Ground Floor Plan

1 toilet
2 liveing room

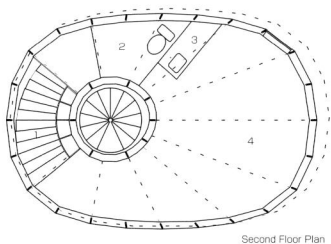

Second Floor Plan

1 stairs-up
2 lavatory
3 kitchen
4 dining room

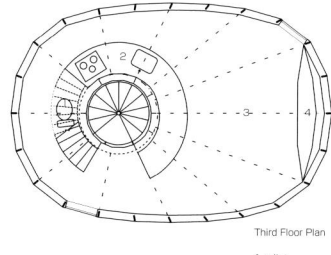

Third Floor Plan

1 toilet
2 kitchen
3 living room
4 rack

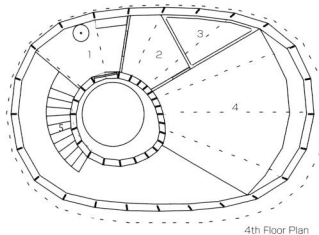

4th Floor Plan

1 lavatory
2 bath room
3 bathtub
4 bed room
5 stairs-up

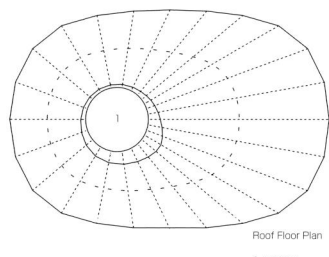

Roof Floor Plan

1 terrace

平面図
螺旋階段を中心にした平面計画。
地階と1階の一部、3階、ロフト階がオーナー住居。
1階と2階が賃貸住居。

Floor Plan
Floor plan design centered on the spiral staircase. Basement and a part of the 1st floor, the 3rd floor, the loft floor is the owner's residence. The 1st floor and the 2nd consists the residences.

Construction - 1

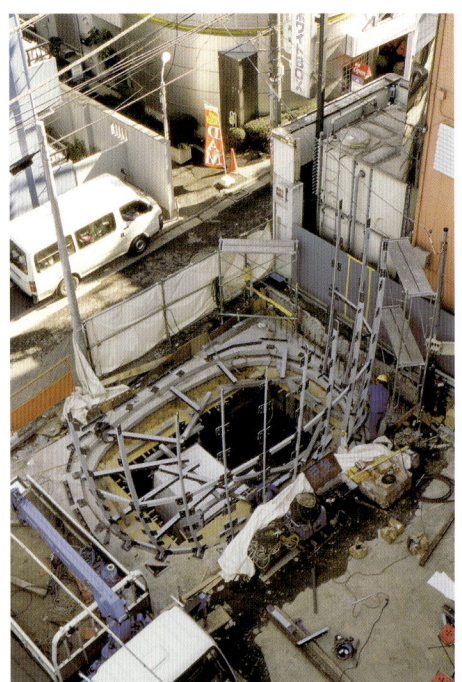

Construction - 2

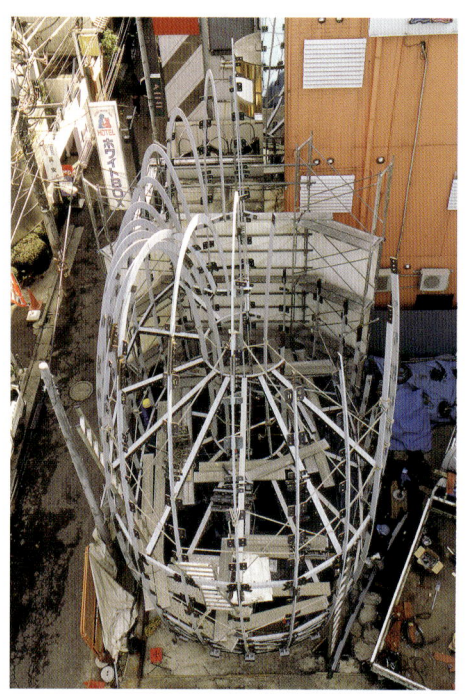

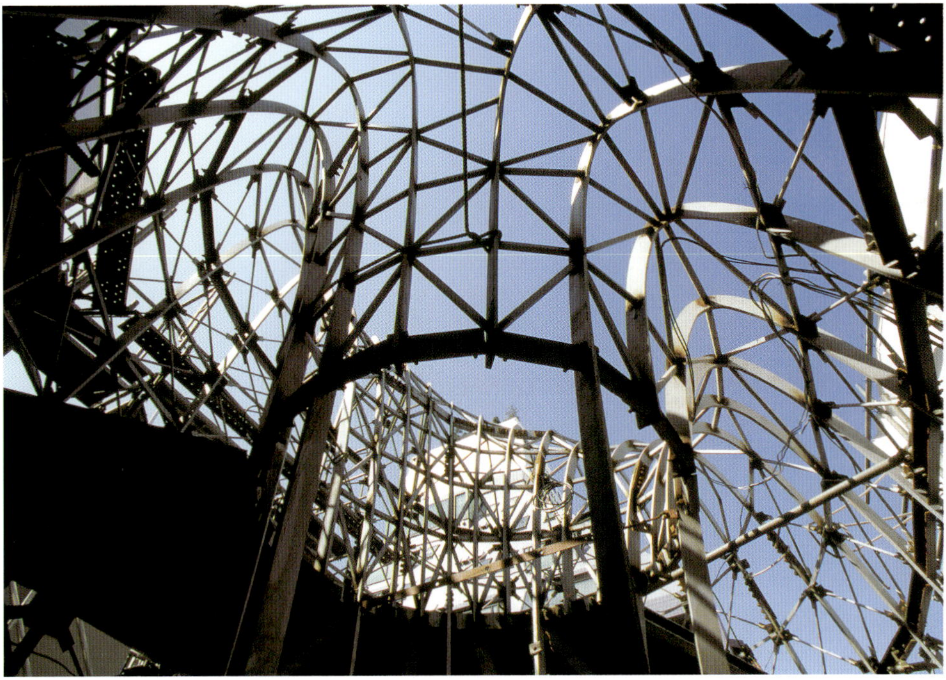

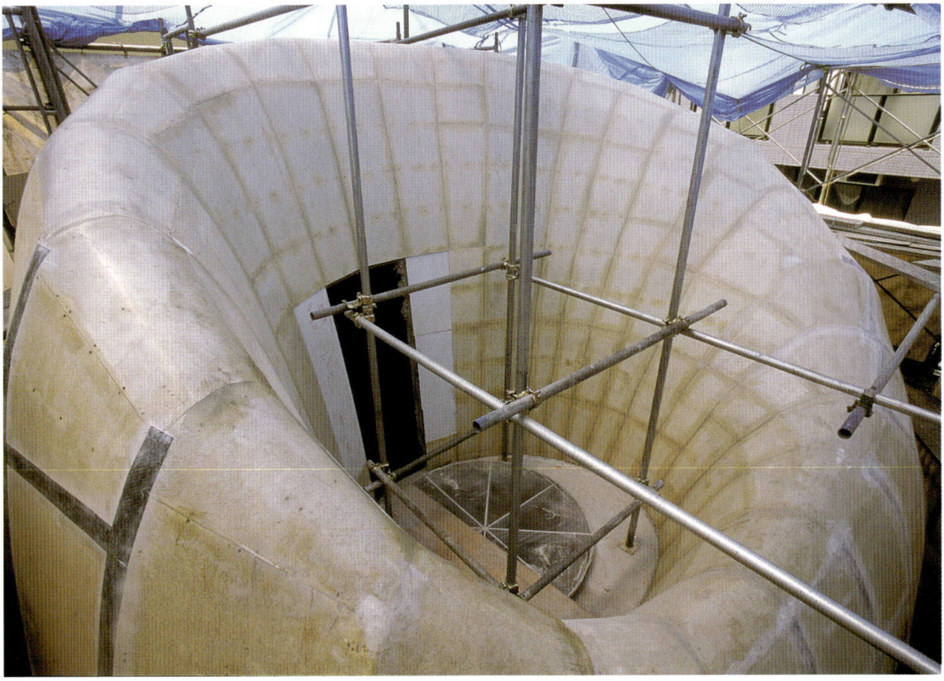

Drawing

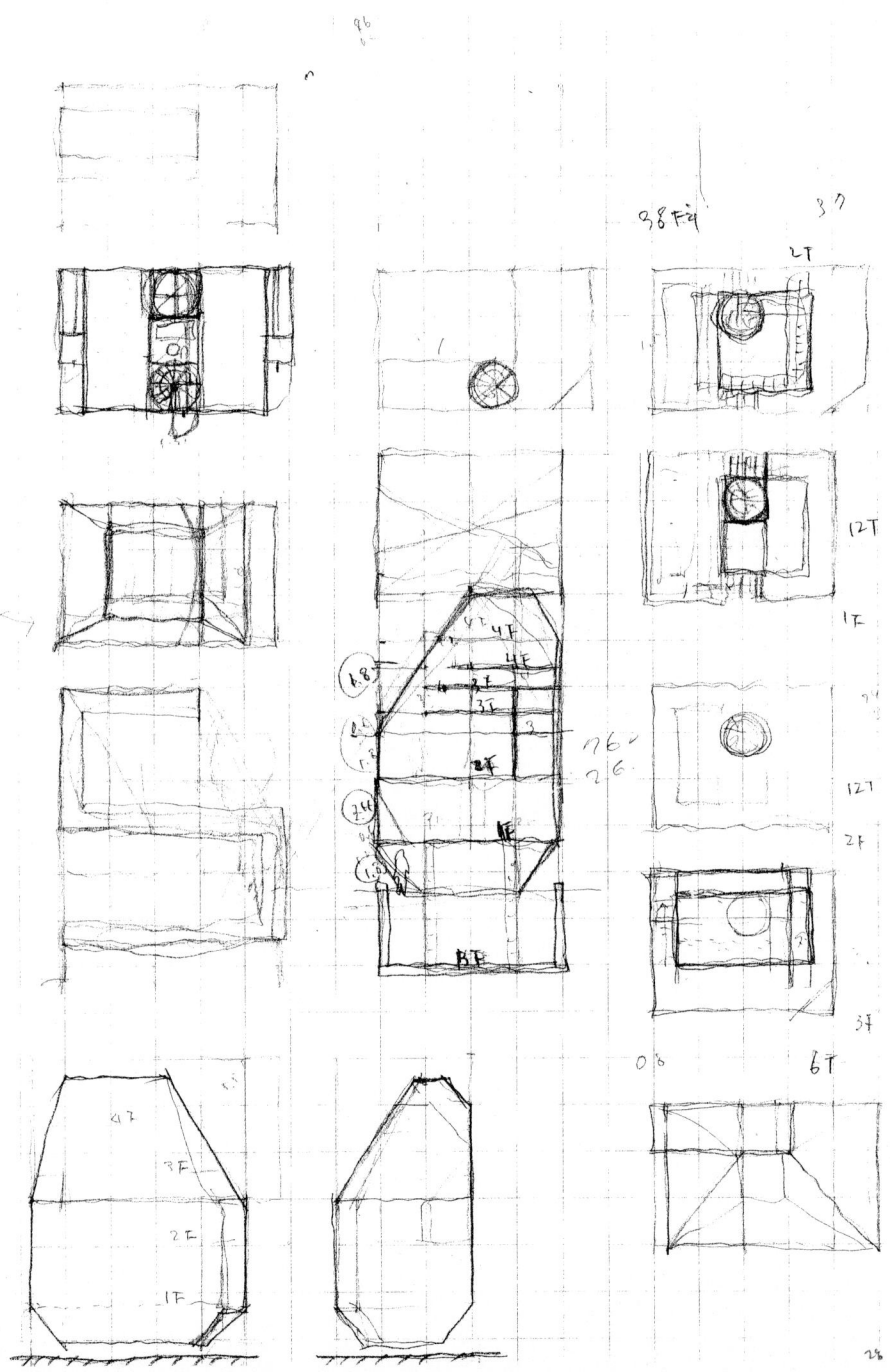

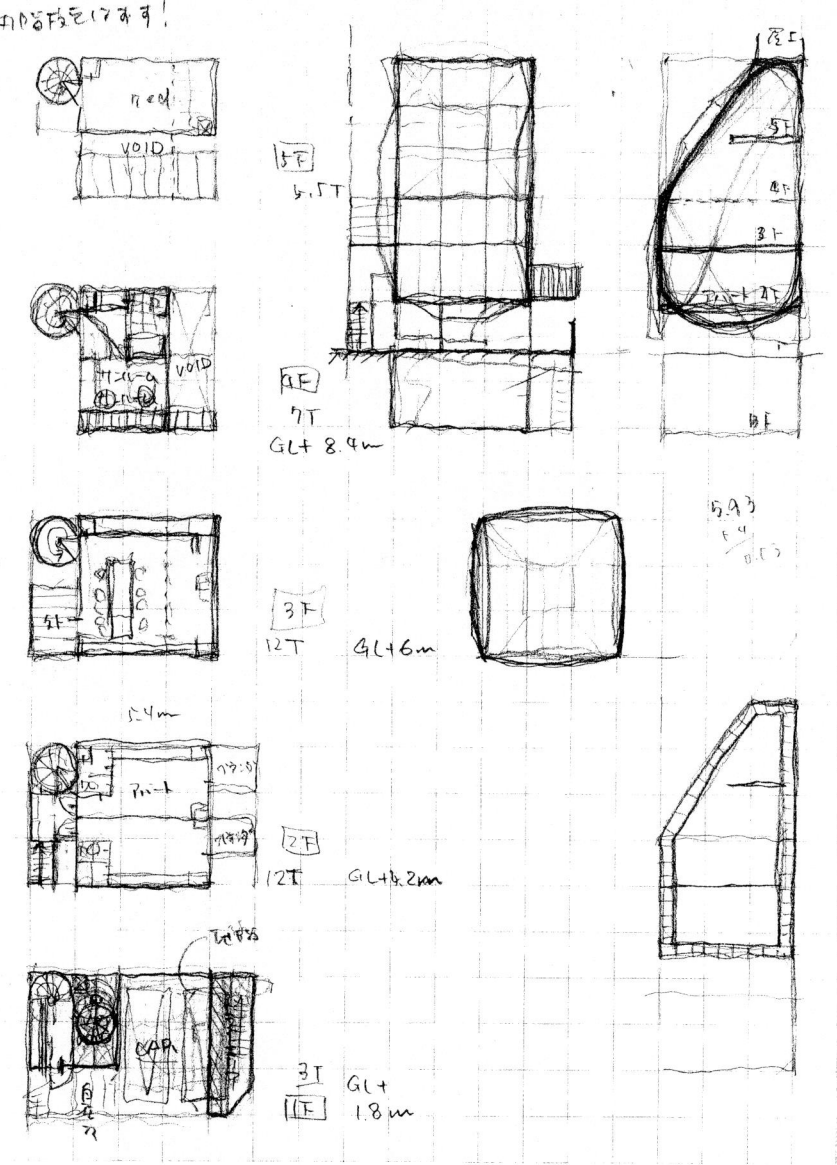

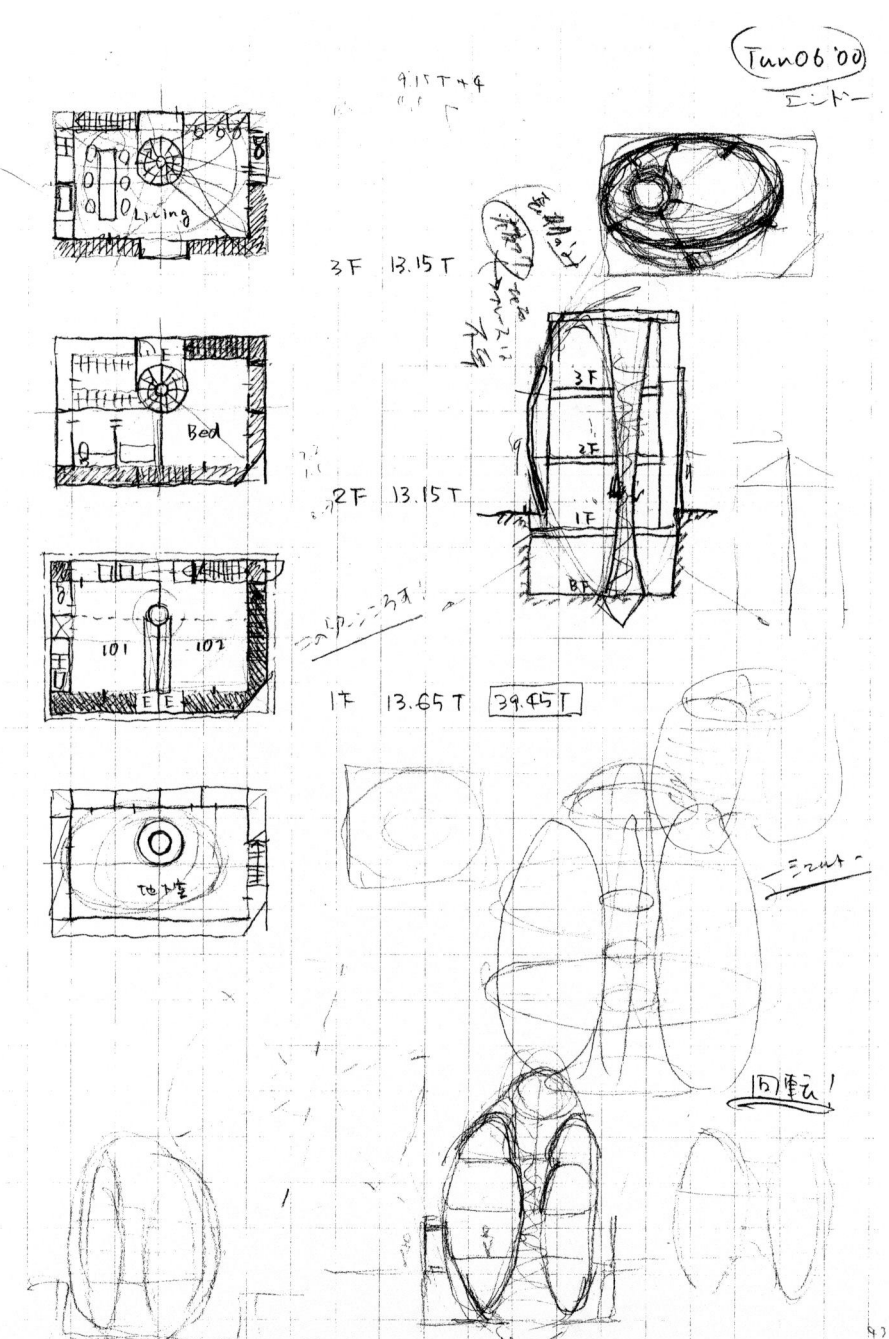

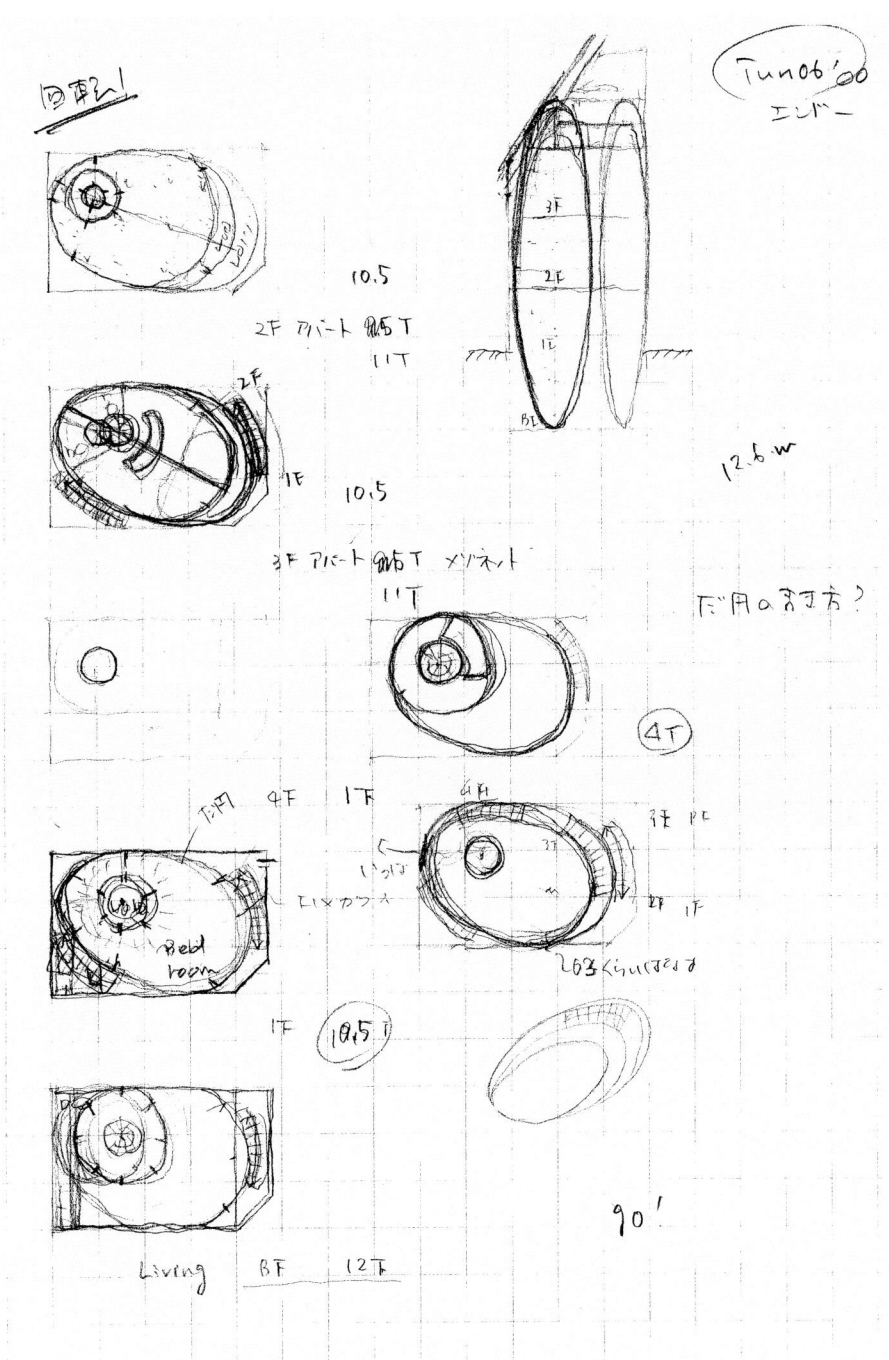

Detail

Skylight Detail

1 mineral board t=9.5+9.5 acrylic emulsion paint finish
2 ventilation
3 column, flat bar-22×100
4 non-inflammable FRP wateproofing, oil paint finish
5 non-inflammable FRP waterproofing, oil paint finish
6 guttering
7 tempered glass t=15mm
8 plaster board t=9.5 acrylic emulsion paint finish
9 guttering
10 sheet waterproofing
11 mineral board t=6+6
12 non-inflammable FRP wateproofing, oil paint finish
13 steel channel 100×50×5×7.5
14 reinforced concrete t=100mm
15 steel channel
16 plaster board t=9.5 acrylic emulsion paint finish
17 sealant
18 steel angle t=1.6
19 acrylic plate t=4.0mm
20 heat insulating materials
21 reinforced concrete t=100mm

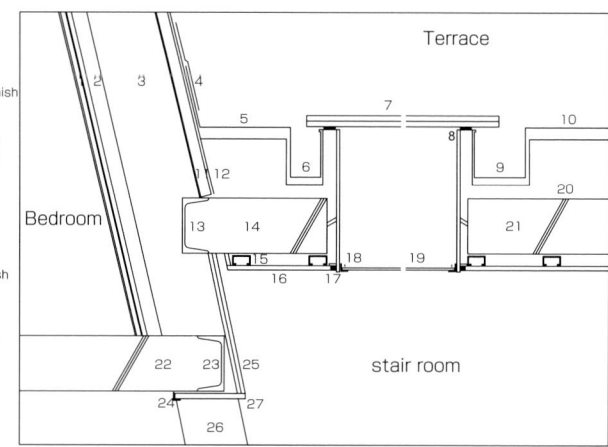

トップライト詳細
FRP塗回しの上に強化ガラス置き。排水は階下のキッチン吊戸棚の中。

Detail of the skylight
Tempered glass is placed on top of the coated FRP, The drain is in the suspended cabinet of the basement kitchen.

開口部詳細
スチール戸と網戸

Detail of the opening
Steel door and screen

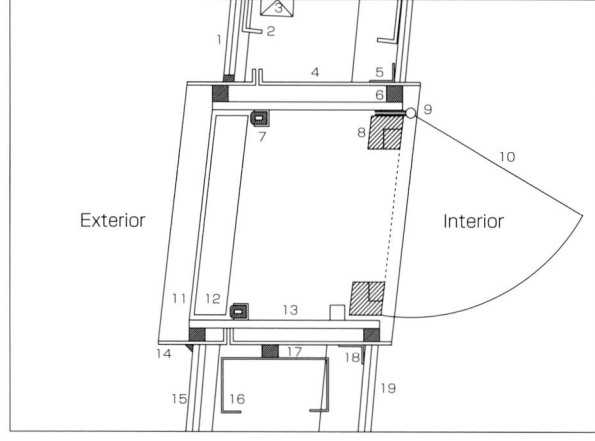

Window Detail

1 non-inflammable FRP waterproofing oil paint finish
2 steel channel 100×50×5×7.5
3 steel square 30×30
4 steel angle t=3.2mm
5 steel angle t=1.6mm
6 sealant
7 steel U-1.6×15×15
8 screen door flame
9 stainless hinge
10 screen door
11 steel angle t=3.2mm
12 steel door t=30mm
13 steel flat bar t=6.0mm
14 steel angle t=3.2mm
15 non-inflammable FRP waterproofing oil paint finish
16 steel channel 100×50×5×7.5
17 steel weld
18 steel plate t=1.6mm
19 mineral board 6 mm × 2 cheesecloth, puttied, acrylic emulsion paint finish

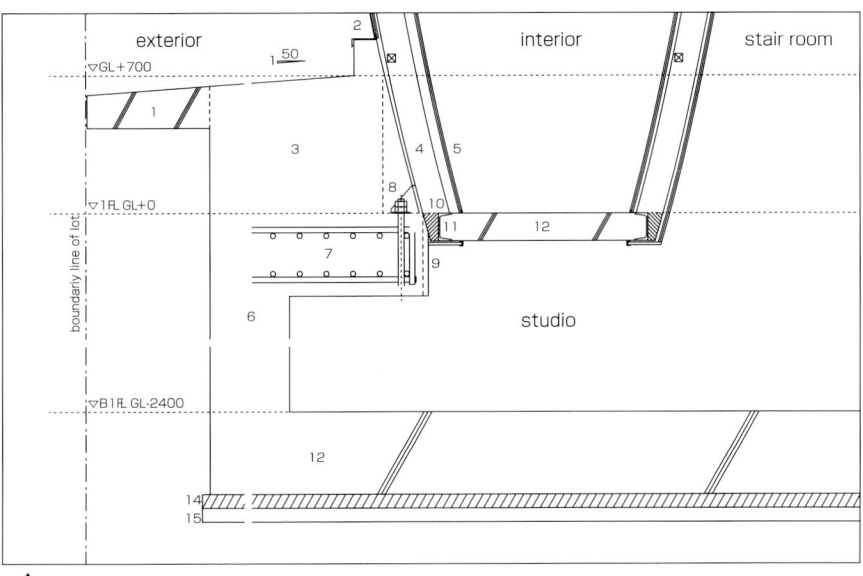

エリップス本体柱脚
矩形の地下室の丸くくり抜かれた穴にエリップス本体がすっぽりと納まっている。

The plinth of the body of the Ellipse
The main body of the Ellipse is completely stored in the round opening dug out from the rectangular basement.

Joint Detail

1 reinforced concrete
2 sheet waterproofing
3 reinforced concrete
4 column, flat bar-22x100
5 mineral board t=6+6
6 reinforced concrete
7 reinforced concrete
8 A.BL 2-M20
9 reinforcing bar D19@200W
10 lebeled concrete
11 steel channel
   100×50×5×7.5
12 reinforced concrete
13 reinforced concrete
   t=300mm
14 lebeled concrete t=50
15 broken stone t=50

小さいこと、東京に住むということ、特殊であること

文：遠藤政樹

　大規模開発された高層ビルの展望台からは、それとは別の東京の風景を見ることができる。一昔前の東京の住宅スタイルは、6,70坪の土地に木造2階建てに柿の木のある庭、というのが一般的であった。バブル崩壊以降は、庭もとれない20坪以下の土地が分譲されている。

　そうした土地に、住宅を構えるには並はずれたエネルギーが必要となる。物理的に土地が小さいため、隣家との関係で窓の位置も自由にできない。土地の価格があまりにも高いため、小さな住宅でさえ、資金調達を工夫しなければならない。都心に住むための総コストは、一般の人が銀行から借りられる金額を超え、例えば、ショップの経営や、貸し部屋の併用を考えるなど、住むこと以外の社会的行為も必要になってきた。それらを解決して、初めて都心に住むことが可能になる。

　つまり、都心に住むということは、終生の家族のための安住場所を求めるだけでなく、いかにして社会や都市と関わりあるものにするかという外向き思考のエネルギーが必要な時代になった。そのため、住宅が、住まい手自らによってプロデュースされなければならないものになってきている。

　建築家にとっても同様である。都心に建つ建築のデザインにかけるエネルギーは変ざるをえないものになった。その敷地固有の狭い解決では、建築が社会資本的役割を担うことはできない。したがって、建築家の個人的な力では解決しきれない問題、例えば、エネルギーをより少なく使う提案、新しい素材、新しい社会スタイル等々のヴィジョンを持った提案を、社会や都市に向かって投げかけなければならないのである。

　結果、個人のアイデンティティによって強く色分けされた一様でない生き生きとした都市、東京がつくられつつある。今、東京中心部では、高層ビルの足元でこうしたことが起きている。

▲ 高層ビルが建ち並ぶ東京の足元には、現在も低層の木造住宅が建ち並ぶ姿が見られる。

At the grounds of the skyscrapers of Tokyo, wooden house can still be seen today.

Being Small, Living in Tokyo and Being Unique
Text by Masaki Endoh

A different point of view of Tokyo is offered from that which can be seen from an observation deck of a skyscraper built as part of a large development project. A generation ago, the typical style of houses was a 200 sqm plot of land with a two-storey wooden building and a persimmon tree in the yard. After the Japanese economic bubble burst, plots were divided and sold for not more than 60 sqm which is too small to live in.

To build a house on that kind of plot requires an extraordinary amount of energy and effort. Because the plot is physically small, one cannot build windows freely due to the closeness of the houses next door and because the cost of the plot is so expensive, it is necessary to be innovative in the means of raising money even for a small house. The total cost of living in the city centre exceeds what most ordinary people can borrow from the bank, therefore for example, and in my own experience, it became necessary for them to think about financial means rather than just living, such as running a shop or subletting a room. Only after these issues are resolved is it possible to comfortably live in the city centre.

We have reached an era where living in the city centre is not only about finding a peaceful residence for the family, but about considering how to make life design interact with society and the city. That means houses are not built by developers as was previously done, but by people, ideas and designs.

This is the same for architects. It has become necessary for them to change the energy spent on the design of buildings in the city centre. The narrow solution for a particular plot of land will not produce architecture that can be considered infrastructure. Therefore, problems that cannot be solved by the architect's individual capacity – for example new ways of using less energy, ideas for new materials and visions of new social styles, etc. – need to be addressed to society and cities at large.

As a result, Tokyo keeps on building itself as a dynamic and un-uniform city, divided by personal identity. Even as we speak, at the center of Tokyo, at the bottom of the towering skyscrapers, vivid diversifications like this are happening.

円山町、エリップスであること

　円山町は、ターミナル駅渋谷に近く、独特な雰囲気を持った土地である。まわりには「ご休憩3800円」という料金表を掲げたラブホテルがずらりと並び、最近は若者向けのクラブも多い。周辺は一種の無法地帯である。世間一般の感覚では、わざわざ住宅を建てようとは思わない場所だ。エリップスはこうした場所に建っている。

　クライアントは、20代後半の若い夫婦。彼らにとって、円山町は、渋谷駅に近く、娯楽から食材から何でもそろう、今までの二人の生活の延長上にある場所である。緑のある郊外で住宅メーカーの住宅を購入することには、リアリティを感じない人たちである。しかし、こうした敷地の建築条件は、通常、法的規制が厳しく、周りの環境状況も厳しく、建物の形は、それによって自動的に決まってしまう。おまけにこの土地は小さく角地である。本来は、目指すべき住まい方があって、それに従って、面積配分、部屋の大きさや配置が決まるはずである。しかし、こうした場所では逆に、都市の持つ状況と条件が動かしがたい大前提となり、生活を追いやってしまう。

　エリップスのユニークな形は、この両方のバランスを釣り合わせる方法を試行した結果である。具体的には、楕円（エリップス）リングの幾何を操作し、それの長軸と短軸の比率を個々に変えて、大きさを変えることによって、都市と住まいをバランスさせた。この住宅を繭のようであるとか、さまざまな形容があるが、ふくらんだ風船のように、住もうとする内圧とそれを規制する外圧が釣り合った状態、それを可能にした形である。実際、この建物のデザインに費やした多くの時間は、その内外のバランスのスタディであった。

　建築は、環境をコントロールするために、面によって囲われなければならない。しかし建築の起源論では、そうした「面」的な「洞窟」と、「線」的な「木の上の小屋」との論争[*1]が続いている。それは、「線」によって建築に、環境のコントロール以外の構築的な思考を、織り込もうとする証である。「線」を連続して「面」にする。リングを回転して3次元形をつくると、どういう展開が期待できるだろうか？

　ポストモダン[*2]以降、私たちが学んだのは形の自立についてである。形は機能の追求の結果だけではなく、それぞれの形の持つ機能の発見、そしてそれに基づいたシステムをつくっていく、その有効性についてであった。「線」で「面」をつくることによって、その二項対立を超えた新しい空間把握術が考えられる。その空間は、明快なものであるが、純粋な幾何でなく、未体験な形で

上: 渋谷駅前。
下: 円山町のホテル街。

Top: In front of Shibuya Station.
Bottom: Hotel street in Maruyama-cho district.

◀ [*1]面「洞窟」と線「木の上の小屋」
人類が創り出した建築の起源を洞窟的な面から構成されるものとして捉えるか、小屋のような線を構成して捉えるかの、論争。

The Planes as a "Cave" and the Lines as a "Hut on a tree".
It is a controversy to wonder about whether if architecture created by the human race was originated from the construction of the plane of a cave or the construction of the line of a hut.

Maruyama-cho – Being an Ellipse

Maruyama-cho is close to the terminal station, Shibuya, an area that has a unique atmosphere to it. In the vicinity, there are "love hotels" with price signs stating, "3800 yen for a rest," and recently you can find many clubs for the young. You could say that this area is a kind of a lawless area. Under normal circumstances, one would not think to build a house here. This is the kind of area in which the Ellipse exists.

The clients are a young couple in their late twenties. For them, Maruyama-cho is close to central Shibuya, is where they can access everything from recreational entertainment to food, and is an extension of their previous lifestyle. They are people who do not find buying a house in the suburbs house surrounded by greenery and sold by builders realistic. However, generally, the building conditions for an area like this are strictly regulated by laws, and the surrounding environmental conditions are also harsh so the shape of the building is automatically decided. Additionally, this plot is small and has corners. Usually there is an ideal lifestyle and a preferred way of allotting area space, so the size of the rooms, their positions and shape of building are decided by these. However, conversely in places like this, the conditions the city holds are priority and make lifestyle the second in importance.

The unique shape of this house is designed after trials of ways to balance out these two criteria: the lifestyle and the city conditions. More specifically, the geometrics of elliptical rings were manipulated, the ratio of the long and short axes were changed, and the shape of the house was considered. This house can be described as a cocoon among other things, but this shape like a blown up balloon made it possible to balance the internal pressure of living and its oppressive external pressure. In actuality, a lot of the time spent on the design of this building was for the study of the balance.

Architecture must be surrounded by planes in order to control the environment, however the continuous discussion between cave "planes" and tree house "lines" in the origin theory of architecture is proof of "lines" being added not for environmental control but to include the will to construct. "Lines" are consecutively placed to make "planes". If you rotate a ring into a three dimensional shape, what kind of formation can you hope to see?

After the post-modern era, we knew about the independence of shapes. This was not only about the results of pursuing function, but was also about discovering the functions of individual shapes and about the validity of creating systems based on those discoveries. By creating "planes" with "lines", a new method of transcending the two opposing ideas about the origin could be reached. The space is lucid,

◀ *2 ポストモダン 装飾を排し機能主義に基づくモダニズム建築に対する反動として現れた。多様性、装飾性などを特徴とする建築群。C・ジェンクスの著書「ポスト・モダニズムの建築言語」から1980年代に流行した。

Postmodernism is defined as the architectural style reactionary to modernism that was characterized by its rejection of ornamentation and which construction was based on functionalism. Post-modernism was characterized by diversity and fanciness. The book "The Language of Post-Modern Architecture" by C.Jencks was very popular in 1980's.

ある。それは、実体的であるが、それがまだ新しいものであるために、観念上の空間でもある。

FRPであること

　通常の建設システムはカルテシアン座標※3に則ってつくられ、それに追従する仕組みがさまざまに用意されている。カルテシアン座標でつくることは、建物の使われ方とは直接の繋がりはなく、構造、材料などの利便性から考えられた結果だ。
　ところで、この建物は、カルテシアン座標にのらない形をしている。そのため、既製品のアセンブルが不可能で、新しい現実化の方法、技術についての再考が必要とされた。そもそもこの建物の形は、スチールのプレート22ミリ厚、幅100ミリの楕円リングを24枚設定し、これを繋ぐことで成立する。それは、非常に説明が単純な形である。しかし、それをひとたび、数式とかモデルといった抽象化の置換作業をしようとすると、とても難しい形となる。見たこともない複雑な数字の羅列となってしまう。
　そうした置換作業を必要としない、単純に形をダイレクトに実物化する方法、そのための技術の使い方を考えることにした。現場施工のFRP材は、こうしたアプローチから決定された素材である。この素材は、ケイカル板下地にガラス繊維を張り、それを樹脂で塗り固めるという現場施工の素材である。
　こうしたモノのつくり方は、技術が先にあってできるスタイルではなく、モノのあり方からはじめて、技術がサポートするつくり方といえる。FRP材は、今まで外壁に用いられることがなかった。プラスチックは燃えやすい素材だからである。その一点さえ解決すれば、シームレスで巨大な不定形の制作を可能にする素材である。新しい技術の導入は、飛躍的に表現の幅と生活の選択の幅を拡げることができる。
　現代はインターネットの時代。情報は、その重要性に関係なく、世の中に溢れかえり、手軽にその情報にアクセス可能な時代である。FRPという素材の可能性にたどり着くことができたのは、実はそうした背景の上に成立している。近代初期の建築家ミース・ファン・デル・ローエ※4が言ったように、「建築家はラテン語を学んだ石工である」必要はもはやない。技術は、情報となってカジュアルな存在になっている。
　具体的なストラクチュアの構成は、楕円リングの強軸方向の座屈止めが床面（盤面）、弱軸方向の座屈止めのブレースが壁面（外皮）となる、個々単独では自立できない仕組みである。部材を互いに連動、機能させ全体となる構成。これは、外部と内部が

※3カルテシアン座標
直交直線座標のこと。
Cartesian Coordinates
Orthogonal and straight line coordinates.

※4ミース・ファン・デル・ローエ
建築家。ドイツ生まれ。(1886-1969)。"Less is more" (無駄な部分を削ぎ落としたデザインが、より豊かなデザインである) という標語で知られ、インターナショナル・スタイルの成立に貢献した近代建築の巨匠。自由な間取りのユニヴァーサル・スペースという概念を提示し、チューゲンハット邸、ファンズワース邸は今でも住宅の珠玉。

Ludwig Mies van der Rohe
Architect. Born in Germany. (1886-1969). Coined the phrase "Less is more". One of the most influential masterminds of the International Style, he praised the concept of the open "universal space", concretized by works such as the Tugendhat House, and the Farnsworth House.

エリップス頂上部。
Ellipse top part.

not pure in geometry, but is a yet to be experienced space. It is realistic, but because it is still new, it also exists only as an ideal.

Being FRP

A usual construction system is built according to the Cartesian coordinates system; in consequence, various systems are also prepared to correspond to it. To build according to the Cartesian coordinates does not relate directly to the way a building is actually lived in, but rather is to take advantage of the conveniences of construction, materials and so on.

This building is in a shape that does not fit on the Cartesian grid. Because of this, the assembly of ready-made goods being impossible, consideration of new methods and technology was necessary. To begin with, the shape of this building is set up with twenty-four 22mm thick and 100mm wide elliptical rings, all joined together. If explained, it is easy to do. However, when one attempts to substitute abstract formulas and models, it becomes extremely difficult. You end up with an enumeration of complex figures.

Such substitution work was judged to be unnecessary, but rather it was more important to think about the development of a technology that can provide a method to directly shape an object. The use of on-site construction of FRP as the material was judged relevant for such an approach. This material enabled site construction by installing the fiber glass on top of the calcium silicate board groundwork, painting it with resin, and hardening it.

Such a way of constructing does not follow the normal pattern of having an original technology and then building according to its capabilities and style, but rather it embodies the way an object should be, and the technology was developed to support its construction. FRP has never been used for exterior walls up to now. The reason for that is because plastic is a combustible material. However if that one point is resolved, it is a material that enables the creation of seamless, huge infinite forms. The introduction of such new technology widens expression and expands the choices of lifestyles.

It is now the age of the Internet. Information overflows in the world regardless of its importance, and it is also an age where this information is easily accessible. It is actually because we are in such a situation that it was possible to discover the possibilities inert in FRP. What was once said by early modern architect, Mies van der Rohe, "The architect is a stone-cutter who had the rudiments of Latin", does not stand true anymore. The understanding and writings of technology exists today as accessible information.

To put the structural system of the elliptical rings concretely, the

等価なダブルコアの形式にあり、クラインの壺[*5]のように内に外を、外に内をもつ構成ともいえる。この構成も、かつてのように、力の負担を明快に分けるようなコア方式といった利便化されたものでない。

スチールであること

　スチールほど開かれた素材はない。
　スチールの特質を応用することでさまざまな表現が可能になり、また限定することで、必要とされるパフォーマンスのみに応えるピュアなシステムをつくることも可能である。この「多様化」と「システム化」。いまだにデザイナーは前者を、エンジニアは後者を追求するものと考えられている。スチールのパフォーマンスを最大現に引き出すのには、この両面について模索が必要になる。私はいつも、その可能性を探ることから出発している。
　「システム化」は、経済性や施工性を見据えた場合、不可欠である。施工性や不特定多数のユーザー要求、敷地条件に容易に反映される許容度の高いものにするためには、建物であるにも関わらず、それは扱いの容易なツールのようなものにまで発展させ、ポテンシャルあるものにする必要がある。それは、パソコンにおけるアプリケーションのようである。それには、物質を可能な限り、単純なルールに支配されるものにまでデザインの範囲を拡げてみなければならない。その結果としてこの建築では、厚さ22ミリの鉛直にたつ楕円リングが24個デザインされた。
　そして、システム化された楕円リングの長軸と短軸の変形とその配置によって、「多様化」を可能にしている。このプロジェクトの場合、敷地のもつ猥雑さや小ささ、これにかかるさまざまな法制限、そしてその中でクライアントの快適に大きく住もうとする欲望、それらの問題に対応できる程のポテンシャルを素材が持った。
　つまり、「システム化」されたものの余白に、「多様性」を位置づけるという、考え方をした。はじめに、あの形がありきばかりではないのである。
　一個人の建築家だからこそできるデザインは、多様性のみを示すことではない。「多様化」と「システム化」を同時にフィードバックさせながらデザインコンセプトをボトムアップさせること。フットワーク軽く、都市の中に違和感なく人工物を併存させること、スチールはそうしたポテンシャルを秘めた素材である。私が行いたいのは、スチールのポテンシャルを利用して、都市空間においてさえ対応可能な、許容度の高いシステムを発明するこ

◀[*5] クラインの壺
ドイツの数学者フェリックス・クラインにより1882年に考案された。メビウスの輪が2次元のテープ状のものをひねり、表を辿っていくとそのまま裏に行き着くものに対し、3次元のチューブをひねり、表を辿ると裏に行き着くようにした立体。

Klein's Bottle
The Klein bottle was first described in 1882 by the German mathematician Felix Klein. The Möbius strip is a two-dimensional strip twisted and merged together at the ends to form a single strip. Similarly, the Klein's bottle is a shape formed from a three-dimensional tube, twisted and merged at the ends.

▲エリップスを形作るスチールの楕円リング。
Steel ring that forms the Ellipse.

buckling of the strong axis is prevented by each slab on each floor. The buckling of the weak axis is prevented by braces on the wall surface (external skin). Therefore without either of which it would not be able to stand alone. This building is composed of synchronizing all members with each other and making the whole. This is where the exterior and the interior both have equivalent value as a double core shape, much like the extroverting of the Klein's Bottle, and where the exterior possesses internal structure. This composition is not a modeled core method to clearly divide the load forces like it was done in the past.

Being Steel

There is no material more widely used than steel.

To make use of the characteristics of steel, many different expressions can be achieved, yet at the same time, limitations from pure systems that respond only to needed performances can also be achieved. This is what is known as "diversification" and "systematization". Though, it is still thought that the designer performs the former and the engineer performs the latter, to maximize the performance of steel, both extremities are needed. So I always aim to bring the two aspects together from the beginning of the design stage.

"systematization" is indispensable to the economy and construction. In order to do that, we need to develop the simple tools that will be able to treat and unleash the potentials of the construction such as building operations, changing user's requests and site requirements. So this is similar to the application of the personal computer. It is governed by simple rules and is easy to use. As a result of this, twenty-four 22mm thick elliptical rings that pass vertically were designed.

And, depending on the changes of the long axis and the short axis of the systemized rings and the rings' placement on the plot, "diversification" was achieved. In the case of this project, it finally has the "potential" to solve these problems of the obscenity and the smallness of the site, the regulations of law and also the client's great desire to live at large. In other words, this unusualness was created after pursuing "systematization". I did not come up with the shape first.

Therefore, architects should not design the "diversification". We should develop "diversification" and "systematization" at the same time, so that we can build the architectures that are well-matched with the society and the city. Steel as a material conceals such high potential. What I wanted to do was to invent a high-tolerance system

とであったのかもしれない。

ナチュラルであること

　私たちは建築を考え、デザインするとき、今までの常識やコモンセンス、あるいは経験から行っている。どんなにプレーンな状態に自分を置こうとも、知らず知らずのうちに限られた枠組みからものを見ている。良い意味でも悪い意味でも、否応なしに、そういった時代や状況に左右されてしまっている。建築はあるコモンセンスのうえに成立しているのであって、この状況を抜きにして有効性についての判断は実のところ難しい。

　建築は常にさまざまな機能（可能性）をもっていて、それがあるシステムに置かれたときに、ある目的にむすびついて機能する（役立つ）。このことが自然＝ナチュラルだとしたら、そのように、もの創りをしたいと考えている。

　そのために、私は初めに、プロジェクトについての基本的な方向性を決め、そこからデザインを始める。このプロジェクトでは、さまざまな検討の結果、先に述べたように楕円＝エリップスという形をどう使っていくかということであった。もちろん、その方針だけで、このプロジェクトをまとめ上げることは不可能である。住むための細かい要求はそうしたものと関係がないし、普通の家具は楕円にフィットしない直角を必要とする。

　そのコンセプトを固守し続ける。すると現実とのギャップが明らかになり、今まで見えていなかった問題が浮上してくる。今までの枠組みでは、暗黙裏に解決されて、目に見えなかった関係が、そうして明らかになってくる。それは、当然プロジェクトを変容させる。私の当初の考え方も変わっていくし、常識にとらわれていた歴史観も変わっていく。その繰り返し、再編成された結果をナチュラルと、私は呼ぶ。

　デザインプロセスは生物の進化プロセスと同じだと考えている。環境に適合するコンセプトが生き残っていく。そうでないものは消え失せていく。そのために私見であるコンセプトは表に出し、環境にもまれるようにしなければならない。

未知なるものへ

　デザインの社会的な意義は、未知なるものがモノにまで形式化されることにある。それは決して紙の上に留まるものではない。事務所設立後の最初の「初台のアパート」(1997) は、具体的な使

in the city by making use of the potential of steel.

Being Natural

When we think of architecture and design, we do so based on general knowledge, common sense or experience. No matter how hard we try to place ourselves on a clean slate, we begin to see things through a limiting framework without realizing. We are influenced by the generation and situation of the times regardless of whether we want to be or not. Therefore it would be difficult to make a valid judgment.

Architecture constantly has various functions (possibilities) and when that is placed within a system, it ties in with an objective and is then able to be useful. If this is the meaning of "natural", in that way I wish to create architecture.

For that reason, I first come up with the basic concept of a project and then start designing. For this project, after much consideration, the concept was decided as being how to use the aforementioned shape of the ellipse. Of course it is nearly impossible to summarize this project using only that concept. Because detailed requests for living have nothing to do with it and normal furniture need perpendicular angles which do not fit in curves.

But I pursue that concept. Then the more that it is kept, the more the balance between the starting point and conservative ideas is realized. I aim to bridge the gap between these two ideas. That is, the adjustment is made, and leads to changing the existing concepts and empirical knowledge of the society and myself. I repeat this throughout the project. That repetition, the reorganisation, is what I call "natural".

I feel that the design process is the same as the process of biological evolution. Design that incorporates new concepts will survive into the future. It is important to constantly challenge the established norms for this architectural evolution to continue.

To the Unknown

The societal purpose of the existence of design is to produce something real from the unknown. That is not at all meant to be something that remains on paper.

The first project after establishing my firm, "Apartment in Hatsudai" (1997), began by moduling the outer wall system without being able to predict exactly how the building would be used. It is similar to the cell division of organisms. The project was carried through discovering the existence of unknowns and resolving them

い方が予め想定されない、外壁システムのモデュール化から始めたプロジェクトであった。生物における卵割のように、漸進的に全体がつくりあげられていき、未知なるものの存在が発見されては解決されていく、そうしたプロジェクトであった。

　現在、私の興味の中心は、技術が単なる建設の手段としてではなく、技術の本来持っている可能性を明らかにすることにある。または、建築以外の人たちと共同でダイナミックに、スキンのような新しい外壁システムを開発することである。どれもが、未知なるものを形にすることにチャレンジすることである。

　近代建築は、それまでの素材や建設方法、思考までを断ち切った新しいモデル化を行い、その繰り返しのうえで発展してきた。しかし問題は、そのモデルの単純性、論理的な飛躍性にある。かつての巨匠と呼ばれる人も例外ではなく、そのモデル化に際しての緻密な探求の必要性を、個人的な美学による解決で封印してしまっている。

　その中でただ一人、その探求を徹底し、モノにまでのフィードバックしたのは、バックミンスター・フラー（1895－1983）[※6]だけであったことを考えると、モデル化とそれへの探求には未解決のまま残されているギャップがまだまだ存在していることが理解できよう。それをこじ開けてはこじ開け、自分が思うように微細な関係づけをすることが必要と考える。

　グレゴリー・ベイトソン（1904－1980）[※7]がいうように、そうした徹底した探求によって、人間の精神や自然世界の構造が次第に明らかになり、サスティナブルな視点で世界をネットワークできるのである。しかしそこには突き進む度量となる構築への意志が必要とされる。技術的にも精神的にも。

　建築家は、偶然性に支配された社会やコンテクストから決して離れずにいる。それは、未知なる他者に対して真正面から向き合い、それを乗り越えるチャンスをもっていることでもある。未知なるものへのチャレンジは永遠に開かれている。

◀ [※6]バックミンスター・フラー
建築家、発明家。アメリカ生まれ。(1895-1983)ジオデシック・ドーム（フラードーム）を発明(1948年)し、彼の思想は現在も影響を与えて続けている。

Richard Buckminster Fuller
Architect. Inventor. Born in the United States. He invented the Geodesic Dome (also known as the Fuller Dome) in 1948, and his thoughts still possesses great influence today.

◀ [※7]グレゴリー・ベイトソン
文化人類学者。アメリカ生まれ。(1904-1980)「精神の生態学」「精神と自然」を著した。

Gregory Bateson
Cultural Anthropologist. Born in the United States. (1904-1980) Author of "Steps to Ecology of Mind" and "Mind and Nature".

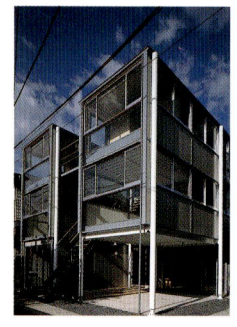

◀ 「初台のアパート」(1997)。

"Apartment in Hatsudai" (1997)

whilst the whole was being created gradually.

Previously, my centre of interest was to view technology simply as a means for construction but now my primary concern is to make known the innate possibilities of technology. Beneath my primary concern lies a secondary aspect, one of which is through dynamic collaboration with people other than architects, to develop a new skin-like outer wall system. These are all channeled to make the unknown into a form in a challenging way.

Modern architecture developed by repeatedly newly modelling in such a way that severed its part from existing materials, methods of construction and even ideas. However, the problem was in the model's simplicity and its theoretical leap. Those who were called masters were not exceptions for they put away the need for detailed pursuit regarding the leap with their own personal aesthetics. Only one of those masters, Buckminster Fuller (1895-1983), did thorough pursuits and even gathered feedback till the end. When considering this, we can understand that there are many unresolved gaps that still exist regarding modelling and its pursuit. We must wrench and open the hidden gap repeatedly, and connect as one line and the world will be connected as we imagine it could be.

As Gregory Bateson (1904-1980) said through, through thorough pursuits is how the human mind and the structure of the natural world are gradually defined, and the world can be networked from a sustainable viewpoint. Then, there must be a progressing amount of will for construction for that.

Architects are never distanced from society or context governed by contingency. This also means that architects directly face the unknown and have the chance to overcome them. Challenges facing the unknown are never-ending and I intend to meet and exceed those challenges in the future.

▶ ジオデシック・ドーム (1948)
バックミンスター・フラー
Geodesic Dome (1948)
Richard Buckminster Fuller

遠藤政樹 ©	Text	© Masaki Endoh
坂口裕康 ©	Photos	© Hiroyasu Sakaguchi
ヘンリー・ツァン ©	Translation	© Henry Tsang
石原秀一	Chief Editor	Shuichi Ishihara
大石雄一朗	Staff Editors	Yuichiro Oishi
馬嶋正司［（株）ポパイ］	Design	Shoji Majima (Popai, Inc.)
（株）シナノ（河野文男　山田厚）	Printer	Shinano, Inc. (Fumio Kono, Atsushi Yamada)

ナチュラルエリップス
建築家　遠藤政樹＋池田昌弘
2006年9月25日発行

Natural Ellipse
Architect: Masaki Endoh+Masahiro Ikeda
25/9/2006

石原秀一	Publisher	Shuichi Ishihara

バナナブックス ©
〒151-0051東京都渋谷区千駄ヶ谷5-17-15
TEL.03-5367-6838 FAX.03-5367-4635
禁無断転載

© Banana Books
5-17-15 Sendagaya Shibuya-ku,
Tokyo, 151-0051 Japan
Tel.+81-3-5367-6838 Fax.+81-3-5367-4635

BANANA BOOKS
PRINTED IN JAPAN
ISBN4-902930-05-6 C3352
落丁・乱丁本はおとりかえします。